A Sun Inside My Chest

Also by Terri Kirby Erickson

Thread Count
Telling Tales of Dusk
In the Palms of Angels
A Lake of Light and Clouds
Becoming the Blue Heron

A Sun Inside My Chest

poems by

Terri Kirby Erickson

Press 53
Winston-Salem

Press 53, LLC
PO Box 30314
Winston-Salem, NC 27130

First Edition

Cover design by Kevin Morgan Watson

Cover art by Stephen White

Cover art photograph by Leonard Erickson

Author photograph by Tanya Odom

Library of Congress Control Number
2020943753

Printed on acid-free paper
ISBN 978-1-950413-30-0

For love

Many thanks to the editors of the following publications where these poems or versions of them first appeared:

Artemis Journal: "The Persistence of Memory"
Birmingham Arts Journal: "The Penguin"
Broad River Review: "Soleá" (Finalist for the Ron Rash Poetry Award)
Christian Century: "Geese," Copyright © 2018 by the *Christian Century*. Reprinted by permission from the August 30, 2018 issue of the *Christian Century*
Deep South Magazine: "Movie Night," "Dragonfly Dance," "The Old Barn"
Dime Show Review: "The Ophthalmology Specialists' Secondary Waiting Room"
Fourth & Sycamore: "Free Breakfast," "Red Dahlias"
Kakalak: "Mid-November," "Heron at Mallard Lake"
Latin American Literary Review: "The River of Doubt"
O.Henry/Salt: "Buttercups," "The Neighbor's Pears," "Four Egrets at the Reservoir," "Summer," "From Our House Behind the Churchyard, After a Storm"
Old Mountain Press: "Surfers," "My Father's Fiat," "The River"
Plainsongs: "Fog" (Editor's Award Poem)
Prime Number Magazine: "Three Turtles"
Red Eft Review: "Ila White"
Redheaded Stepchild: "In Response to a Black and White Photograph of Robert Frost"
Sandy River Review: "Morning Music"
Sleet Magazine: "The Knife Sharpener's Chickens"
The Mantle: "Mockingbirds"
The Sun: "Loving You Burns Like Shingles"
The Sunlight Press: "Branch Point Fridays" (Nominated for Pushcart Prize), "Red Berries"
Turtle Island Quarterly: "New Bathing Suit"
Valparaiso Poetry Review: "Albino Opossum"
Whole Terrain: "The White Mountains in Early June"

Contents

Three

Four

Five

Six

Author's Note

A few weeks after this manuscript was completed, my mother died unexpectedly. Six months prior to her death, my father passed away. Tom and Loretta Kirby were high school sweethearts, married sixty-three years.

Intellectually, we know if we live long enough, our parents will die. But until it happens, until you lose them, there remains some part of you that believes your mother and father are immortal.

So, the grief and shock that follows the death of a parent is like no other. Yet, there is no doubt in my mind that love lives on, like a sun inside us, filling our hearts with warmth and light.

I therefore dedicate this collection of poems, *A Sun Inside My Chest*, to "love"—*agape, storge, phileo*, and *eros*, as well as love for the natural world—because what else matters, in the end, more than who and what we have loved?

Terri Kirby Erickson
February 2020

The sun is new each day.

—Heraclitus

One

Loving You Burns Like Shingles

My love for you is a sun inside my chest.
It burns like shingles, wrings tears from my eyes
like the hands of a tough old woman washing
clothes in a tin tub. You're as toxic as poke salad,
your words a swarm of bees. You haunt me
like a chain-clanking ghost, yet I welcome you
like the mailman. You're a zeppelin in disguise,
the zip line to disaster. I need you like bad brakes,
a stick of dynamite, loose bricks in the walk.
But step into a room and my heart bumps its mouth
against the bowl of my ribs like a starving
goldfish. You scissor-cut my will, turn my brain
to shredded wheat. Look at me once, and my pot
begins to boil. Look at me twice, and the dog
of my desire becomes a junkyard beast—
though the feral cat in me hungers
to call your body *home*.

Weeping Willow

When the great leviathan of dark clouds thunders
across the sky, dragging its thin, gray sheet

of rain, and the wind whistles like a freight train,
as lonesome and pure as a coyote's

call, the willow tree's branches lift like the arms
of women wearing green dresses—reaching

for something they have lost. And after the storm,
tears drip from its slender leaves,

and the tremble in its trunk is like an earthquake
that insects, scurrying up and down

its deeply furrowed bark, can feel—and a single
starling, just now beginning to sing.

Geese

Canada geese, after leaving Mallard Lake,
are walking uphill, their webbed feet
like flippers flapping beneath the wetsuit
of their bodies. They move like heavyset
ladies who have lifted their curvaceous
selves from a swimming pool, fulsome
and luscious in their beauty. They walk
in single file as if queuing up for some-
thing so wonderful, it is worth the wait.
But it's the same old grass, the same old
hill, though leaning over it are trees, and
from the trees fall leaves through which
the sun shines, turning every leaf to gold.
And the lake they left behind continues
to beckon, so many will soon turn back
to it—its mirrored surface reflecting the
scudding clouds and limbs not yet barren
of their once-bountiful foliage. And all
the while, the geese honk as if they are
irritable drivers stuck in traffic, yet they
can take flight any time, and some do,
leaving behind the hill, the trees, the lake,
their fellow travelers—everything that
holds them to the ground. Because even
when geese fly in formation, each goose
takes off alone, flapping its own wings,
finding its place in a vast expanse of sky
where even a solitary bird separates the
waters above the earth from the waters
below, as necessary and important to this
world as anything God has ever made.

Ila White

In the dark dresser drawer my grandmother, Ila
White, slept as if she were still in the womb,

an infant so small, she fit in her father's palm.
Three babies ahead of her died before birth

and another one, soon thereafter. *We won't lose
this child*, my great-grandmother, Nannie, said,

opening the drawer and tucking her daughter in.
Baby Ila's kidney-bean-lungs might have held

a thimble-full of air, and her cry was a mewling
sound, like a newborn kitten. But her mother

heard it clear across the barnyard; the cow she
was milking bellowing at the loss of her warm

hand on a cold morning as Nannie kicked over
the wooden stool, grabbed the bucket, and ran.

The Ophthalmology Specialists' Secondary Waiting Room

Light is gentle here, and scarce—a room
designed for dilated pupils, for patients
with glaucoma, cataracts, and macular
degeneration—people whose eyes have
somehow failed them. Several wear dark
sunglasses. Others blink and blot their
eyes with tissues. At various times, every
chair is taken. Then, a name is called, and
after that, another. But no seat is vacant
for long. There are so many of us, and so
few hours left in the day. While we wait,
some engage in whispered conversations.
We compare eye pressures, past surgeries,
and treatments, share stories like cowboys
gathered around a circle of slowly dying
embers—though most people sit in stoic
silence, watching the wall-mounted TV,
checking their cell phones, or staring into
space. One elderly woman leans over her
walker and shouts, *She*, pointing to her
middle-aged daughter, *keeps shushing me*.
And when her daughter says, with harried
affection, *Shhh*, most can't help but smile,
faces illuminated like priceless paintings by
the faintest, yet unbearably beautiful, light.

Albino Opossum

Moon-marked, a bloated, bone-white marsupial
lay still in the road. No more lumbering through
the tall grass, snout-first, its pale belly dragging

the ground like a choir boy's cassock. Solitary,
nomadic, and different since birth from its sisters
and brothers, this pallid possum stepped alone

onto the asphalt, claws clicking until it keeled
over as opossums will when frightened, and never
got up. There wasn't a mark on it from the metal

beast that barreled into its body, only a mound
of milky fur—its mouth, the pale pink of ballet
slippers, baring all fifty of its sharp little teeth.

The Old Barn

So cold, you can see your breath in the old
barn, and sunlight slips through the narrow
spaces between slats. Spiders have looped
their sticky webs like makeshift curtains
around the dirt-smudged windows, and the
air smells of cow dung and hay, both scents
hoof-stamped so deep into the floorboards,
nothing short of burning will get them out.
But it is peaceful here, among the ghosts
of livestock past, behind the house with its
caved-in roof and cramped, mouse-infested
rooms for which the word *abandoned* comes
to mind. But nothing says *defeat* in the barn.
It was built to last and it has lasted. Listen
and you will hear the echoes of well-fed cattle
lowing, the purr of a milk-whiskered barn cat,
the footsteps of a farmer's wife, the squeak
of her metal pail. The heart of this home was
here and it goes on beating when all else has
failed, when the money is gone and the family
has long since moved away. The fields may
be fallow, the ruts in the road beaten down by
cars that pass by rather than turn in, but the
barn remains, sturdy as the day it was raised,
doors open like a mother's welcoming arms.

Dragonfly Dance

After days of rain, the clouds lift and a cluster
of dragonflies hovers, then zigs

and zags through the moisture-laden air.
Their wings beat faster than a helicopter's blades,

and their bodies shine like drops of water in dusk's
final display of light. It is a brutal dance

of predator and prey, smaller insects so swiftly
devoured by the marauding mob,

we never see them. But in minutes, the dragonfly
feeding frenzy is done

and clouds gather over the house again, like old
men wearing dark jackets—and we

are left with the memory of iridescence, the hum
of a thousand dragonfly wings departing.

Free Breakfast

The Springhill Suites free breakfast area
was filling up fast when a man carrying his
disabled young son lowered him into his
chair, the same way an expert pilot's airplane
kisses the runway when it lands. And all the
while, the man whispered into his boy's ear,
perhaps telling him about the waffle maker
that was such a hit with the children gathered
around it, or sharing the family's plans for the
day as they traveled to wherever they were
going. Whatever was said, the boy's face was
alight with some anticipated happiness. And
the father, soon joined by the mother, seemed
intent on providing it. So beautiful they all
were, it was hard to concentrate on our eggs
and buttered toast, to look away when his
parents placed their hands on the little boy's
shoulders and smiled at one another, as if
they were the luckiest people in the room.

The Knife Sharpener's Chickens

The knife sharpener's chickens scatter like pool
balls in his narrow front yard, caught between
the sound of sharpening and the revving motors

of adolescent boys showing off minimal driving
skills. Their days seem to be spent, for the most
part, sprinting from tree to tree, squawking, and

foraging for meals on the run. Though ignorant,
we assume, of chicken mortality, knives scraping
against whetstones and the whine of tires on the

busy road, keep the hens in a near-constant state
of hysteria. Only when the sun goes down, does
the sound of sharpening cease and the traffic slow

long enough for the birds to sleep—at least until
first light, when patrons begin to pull into the dust-
covered driveway, brandishing their dull blades.

Summer

Bee-stung, stringy-haired girl with a belly full
of grape Kool-Aid, banana popsicles, and

watermelon seeds too small to spit out—you
are born again every summer into the body

of a woman you never met and wouldn't speak
to if you had, with a mother who drove *don't*

talk to strangers into your head like a roofing
nail. I can feel you rising up in me come June,

like a cornstalk pushing through hard ground.
Because of you, I want to climb every tall tree

like a bear cub, find a hot metal slide and scoot
down it, sticky and squealing. I want dirt on my

heels, sugar on my tongue. So I eat cake for
breakfast, go barefoot to get the morning mail.

New Bathing Suit

My friend is wearing her new black bathing suit.
It came with the proper cups, made to fill
with one breast and the memory
of another—which is not to say *emptiness*—
but the fullness that comes to us, with sacrifice.
There is no one more alive than she is now,
floating like a lotus or swimming, lap after lap,
parting the turquoise, chlorine-scented water,
her arms as sturdy as wooden paddles.
And when she pulls herself from the pool,
her new suit dripping—the pulse is so strong
in her wrists and throat, a little bird
outside the window will hear it, begin to flap
its wings to the beat of her heart.

Two

Jubilee

"A jubilee is an upwelling of water from the floor of the bay to the surface. Bottom-dwelling creatures...are carried up... to the shallow water of the beaches."
—*History Daily*

Jubilee! Jubilee! cries the barefoot boy, splashing
through the bathwater-warm surge of high tide.
People carrying buckets, nets, gigs, and washtubs
rush toward a mass exodus from the murky deep,
of blue crab, shrimp, flounder, stingrays, and more,
to the sandy shores of Mobile Bay. Crustaceans by
the hundreds, pinchers waving, are climbing over
teeming piles of slippery carapaces, only to wind
up steamed, ice-cooled, and swallowed by tourists
and locals alike. And for days afterward, the oily
odor of deep-fried flounder will hover over Mobile
in a thick, lip-smacking haze. What a gift to receive
the earth's bounty with such little effort on our part,
though some might say a starved soul is not so easily
filled. For now, however, we won't speak of hungers
left unsated by fresh seafood seasoned with paprika,
salt, and bay leaves, served on platters with a lemon
wedge and sprigs of forest green parsley, or straight
from the pot or pan—not while our barefoot herald
is harvesting fist-sized shrimp, his face still radiant
with joy and the roseate blush of a jubilee dawn.

Four Egrets at the Reservoir

Four great egrets,
the wands of their
slender necks waving,
wade through tall
reeds and tranquil
water to the sound
of a kingfisher's
call. The tops of
surrounding trees
are lit from above,
the ground below
them shadowed.
All is serene, from
a gander swimming
in circles to water
striders skating
across the reservoir's
still surface. In
summer, lilies
bloom and multiply,
their petals a delicate
shade of pink. But
the wedding-veil-
white of an egret's
feathers is stark
in early spring
against umber,
sienna, and olive—
and the evening air
is cool and weight-
less here, where egrets
come and go—like
darkness and the light.

My Father's Fiat

In our father's red Fiat, a brief indulgence
soon traded for a more family-friendly,
earth-tone, four-door sedan, my brother
and I were squeezed into a compartment
behind the front seats, and our mother sat
up front, her auburn hair swirling around
her perfect face. Balls of twine are less
loosely packed than the four of us in that
tiny two-seater, but how Dad must have
loved tooling around, top down, in a red
convertible, as if he wasn't a mortgage-
bound, hard-working husband and father,
but a young man without a worry in the
world, fresh as a new dress shirt. But with
a couple of giggling kids in back, and close
beside him, his wife holding her wide-
brimmed, church-going hat with a white-
knuckled grip, perhaps those Sunday after-
noon drives seemed less like a devil-may-
care jaunt, and more like how it feels to be
a train conductor, responsible for every soul
onboard—his foot so light on the gas, we
should still be riding in Dad's last single
man's car, making our way back home.

Buttercups

Let loose in the pasture, bays, chestnuts, grays,
and paints graze beneath blue skies, their coats

shining like copper pots. And scattered around
their feet, creeping buttercups, yellow as freshly

grated lemon zest—each petal clustered around
the center, creating a corolla of color so dazzling

they rival the sun's golden light. And it is quiet
here, the way a room is quiet but not silent, with

the sporadic whinnies and wickers of contented
horses, the buzzing of bees, the croaking of frogs

in a nearby creek—a low hum of pleasing sounds.
But it is mostly about the light, this idyllic scene,

how bright it shines on a horse's satiny skin, how
all the flowers cup their yellow palms to catch it.

The Rookery

In the boughs of the tallest tree alongside a muddy
river, is a rookery with six nests of miniature blue
herons. They clack like wheels on a railroad track,

the sound of their starvation an urgent call to parents
that appear, one by one, to feed their frantic young.
For some, the nest has grown cramped and crowded,

each baby bird jockeying for the best position. Others
are newly hatched from azure eggs, their fuzzy heads
peeking over sticks and twigs jutting in all directions.

Meanwhile, the wind blows with just a hint of chill,
and branches rock like cradles as the sun bestows its
benevolent warmth on the great blue herons and the

rustling leaves and the river's russet water flowing
toward the sea. And it seems as if every living thing
is busy doing what it was made to do, and the world

is a perfect place for baby birds, their hunger sated
as they sleep beneath a cloudless sky—the light just
now beginning to fade, loosening its grip on the day.

Morning Music

First, my sleeping husband, his slow
and steady

breathing. Then, through an open
window, the sound of rain

running across the lawn, its silver
slippers soft as ballet shoes.

After that, crickets and a neighbor's
barking dog.

And finally, like the favored soloist
in a choir, a cardinal

repeats the same two notes again
and again as dove-gray

light shines through every drop
of rain and shimmies

around our room as if the day,
still in the arms of night, is dancing.

The Last Leaf

The sapling's last leaf, as red as the first
countertop in my parents' kitchen, or an apple
at its pinnacle of ripeness,

flutters in the wind. It is the size of a small
child's hand and hangs from a branch as slender
as a vein—bare of every leaf,

save one. With a snap, however, of a sapling's
slim fingers, it will drift like a feather
to the ground. But see how the light

shines through its trembling blade, revealing
the leaf's reluctance, like all the rest
of us, to let go.

Porch Light

A widow, whose farmhouse
sits in a field of wildflowers, turns her porch
light on and goes to bed. It glows
like a supernova in the inky darkness
of the flatlands. She never bargained on a solitary
life, seeing no one but a boy on his bicycle,
bringing groceries, mail, and newspapers.
She likes the sound of his wheels on the gravel
drive, his cheery hello, but isn't sad when he is gone.
Alone day and night, she is never lonely.
She sleeps from dusk to dawn without waking.
Strange how a single light is such a comfort.
She imagines that little bulb burning the sky's
dark fabric like the scorch of a hot iron
on her husband's shirts, its incandescent shine
so clear and bright, pilots flying low can see
it on their way to somewhere else.

Eating Watermelon

Eating watermelon from a plate on my dining room table
is not the same as skipping around my grandparents'
backyard, taking bites from a half-moon slice. I can still

feel that sugary juice running down my chin, taste flecks
of salt from my grandmother's plastic shaker on the
watermelon's soft and crunchy flesh. I am tidier with it

now, scooping the fruit from the rind and spooning it into
my mouth, neat as a cat. And while this summer treat tastes
much the same, I miss running through the tall grass with

my ruby treasure, spitting seeds and taunting my brother—
long gone from this world—that my piece is bigger than
his. I miss my grandparents, too, and my parents' youth

and happiness, unbroken by loss and grief. So I sit at the
table alone, swallowing bite after bite of my childhood,
licking salt from my lips—the bitter mixed with the sweet.

Heron at Mallard Lake

Framed by a semicircle of cement,
a great blue heron stands in shallow

water beneath a stone bridge. Light
pools on either side, though the heron

is in shadow, its slim silhouette barely
discernable from the mottled back-

drop of Mallard Lake. So still, this
muted bird could be a painting. Then

it lifts one spindly leg after the other,
which looks to me, like a miracle of

animation—as if God is breathing life
into the heron's narrow body and after

that, its massive wings. Flapping, the
heron flies to the sun-soaked shore,

darkness falling from its feathers as it
lands there, like another beam of light.

In Response to a Black and White Photograph of Robert Frost

You, with an ax resting on your shoulder,
your shock of white hair. I like the wool
coat, your casual working-man's shirt.
Your weathered barn, the yard plastered
with snow—even the tree-lined horizon,
waiting for you to trudge toward it—is the
perfect backdrop for a picture. And if words
are circling your brain, looking to land on
a poem, they are as good before you write
them as they will be afterward. But first,
there are chores to finish and breakfast to fix,
perhaps someone sitting across from you at
the table, upon whom your gaze will happily
rest. Yet, you have stopped what you were
doing long enough to pose, your impatience
to be gone not quite contained. You long to
turn your rugged face, with its artful lines
and heavy brows, toward the tasks at hand.
Beyond this, the public is not allowed to
know or to ask—only to read what you will
write by a snow-lit window or wherever your
body settles—perhaps a favorite chair next
to a fire, burning the wood you have cut.

The Neighbor's Pears

The last of the pears dot the neighbor's
yard, their taut green skins giving way
to brownish pulp. Yellow leaves flung

from wind-tossed branches scud across
our lawns like golden clouds—the sun's

slim rays a decoration, a bit of gilding
with no real warmth. It seems the time
has come when all of life seeks its place

before the soil hardens beneath a skein
of frost and pale blue skies turn gray.

Even pear trees go dormant, dreaming
of budburst and blossoms—little green
bells swinging again, from every limb.

Three

Les Guinguettes de Robinson

Let's pretend we are in Paris at *Les
Guinguettes de Robinson*, a bar built
in the branches of a chestnut tree—
the moon like a communion wafer,
unbroken. We, too, are whole, our
bodies like new instruments barely
lifted from their cases, our lives un-
sullied yet, by sorrow. High above
the rain-washed streets, among the
rustling leaves and limbs, our hands
reach for one another like couples
in crowded train stations, to keep
from being parted. But tonight, at
Les Guinguettes de Robinson, there
are no hordes of travelers carrying
heavy suitcases—only lovers, and
we are weightless, so light we must
have floated to our tables, so much
in love, even the air tastes like wine.

Daylilies

At last the daylilies have bloomed
and are reaching out from the steep bank
like beggars pleading for alms.

With only one day to shine, these diurnal
darlings are hungry for everything—
sunlight, rain, bees, butterflies—

although, as one blossom fades, another
blooms, so the lilies appear to live
all summer. Their tangerine-tinted petals

are as vibrant as traffic cones, with slim,
blue-green leaves. And each flower
is as solitary as a single pilgrim

on its brief journey from morning to night.
Yet, every bloom is connected
to the buds and flowers and foliage

and roots, of the same plant—
and by dying, makes room for the lovely
golden-throated lilies yet to come.

Movie Night

Fresh from our baths and clean as a pair
of brand-new whistles, my brother and I,
dressed in cotton snap-top pajamas, rolled
around the backseat of the family station
wagon like a couple of *aggies* (nobody
wore seat belts in the sixties) all the way
to the Winston-Salem Drive-In. It wasn't
long, though, before the asphalt-flavored,
summer-singed freeway air yielded to the
scent of dry grass, fry grease, and dime
store perfumes favored by teenaged girls
whose tan shoulders seemed permanently
bowed by the heavy, muscle-bound arms
of slick-haired boys filling their fathers'
Dodge Darts, Plymouth Furies, and Ford
Fairlanes with enough cigarette smoke to
preserve a side of beef. But all we cared
about—once our father attached that silver,
static-spitting speaker to the driver's side
window and Mom handed out treats from
home—was what happened on the screen
where giant heads, surrounded by stars,
moved their lips to the hiss and pop of dis-
embodied voices ricocheting around our
car like ghosts, looking for something lost.

Cadillac Mountain

Far above the rocky shores of Mount Desert Island,
we stand on Cadillac Mountain—the sea below us
bluer than the bluest sky—with smaller islands rising

from the water like whales breaching the surface
to breathe. The morning sun heats our heads and faces,
but the air is brisk and the wind blows in rhythmic

gusts as if this mountain is a ship sailing into a storm.
Children clamor over the stones, the sounds of their
laughter blown like silt that settles among the green

alder and goldenrod, flat-topped asters and sheep laurel.
In a land carved by glaciers, people are as transient
as butterflies. Yet, we leave behind stories and songs

and poems for others to find—the miracle of our lives
like sails furling and unfurling, while rocks go on and
on, puncturing the soil and piercing this radiant sea.

Marisol

Woman of the tossed plates and brandy
snifters,

the shrine to baby Jesus in your bedroom,
the lit candles—

you fed our childhood with your platters
of fried plantain,

your *arroz con pollo.* Your voice, raised
or lowered, was our neighborhood's

music, your children our dearest friends,
our secret crushes.

Even the street misses you—the tap, tap
of your tapered heels—

your house more empty now than shoes
you stepped out of, dancing.

Hoot Owl

Hello again, my yellow-eyed friend, purveyor
of omens for good or ill. Your heavy body bends
the branch, and your *hoot* is like a foghorn

blowing across the night-drenched field where
voles lie trembling in the sun-scorched grass.

As I stand by my open window, listening, the full
moon's light washes over my upturned face

and the humid air is rushing into the house like
water on a ship at sea, but I don't want this song

of yours to end. It speaks to a wildness in me
that is like a fire, burning. You declare my yard

to be your own and I am happy to share it, to
dream of flying over the woods and fields with

a cry that lives in my lungs and throat finding
release at last—the hunger for everything sated
because as long as night lasts, it is mine.

Lemon Salad

Near the Gulf of Solerno, a woman wearing
a bright yellow dress carts a basket of lemons
up a stone staircase. I can see her in my mind's
eye—her face ruddy and wrinkled by the hot
sun—and all the little suns resting in a basket
she carries on top of her head, which makes
the journey easier given her sturdy shoulders
and a neck her mother used to say, is as thick
as a bull's. To her husband, however, she is
lovelier than the sunrise as she walks toward
him with her basket of fruit, a few of which he
will thinly slice and place in a single layer on
a chipped blue plate. He drizzles each circle of
citrus with olive oil, seasons them with pepper
and salt. Then they will dine beneath a *platano*
tree in their own front yard, just as they have
done for many decades—toothless and happy.

Nine Piglets

Nine piglets—no mother pig in sight—
have formed a conga line in a neighbor's

front yard. So black they could have been
created from the spaces between stars,

their bellies are as plump as foie gras-
fattened ducks, and their coats shine like

newly polished dress shoes. They conga
nose-to-tail, squealing with porcine glee

the way a child, free of supervision, might
do. They pay no mind to the cars zooming

by as they make their way across the gravel
driveway, one pig following close behind

the other like climbers on a narrow ledge,
while shadows from surrounding trees,

drawn with the same dark ink, vanish into
the blackness of their nine, bovine bodies.

At the Nu Wray Inn

founded in 1833

At the Nu Wray Inn in Burnsville, North Carolina,
the wooden floor creaks and the lobby door is open
or closed, depending on the time of day. The front
desk is empty, as if the inn is running itself, and the
light is so dim, a shy spirit could find respite there,
from its ghostly glow. And music plays sometimes,
its source a mystery—the songs from an era so long
ago, few among the living could name the tunes.
A decades-old fridge, cooling its unfilled innards,
sits by a flight of floral-carpeted stairs, and a blaze
has risen so many years from the stone fireplace,
we can almost hear the tick, tick of logs burning,
though the inner hearth is dark in summer, and the
wing-backed chairs turned away. And through the
doors of an upstairs parlor full of antique sofas and
old paintings, a plank porch invites guests to survey
the verdant square, the cars passing by, and people
out walking. Abandoned bird nests nestle against
paint-peeled columns, which look to be the safest
spots in town for raising chicks. And every guest-
room features a different decor, some facing the
busy street, others a fragrant garden. But best of
all is when the night, like a soft blue shawl, settles
over Burnsville and its ring of mountains, and how,
if we listen closely, we can almost hear the scratch
of Thomas Wolfe's pen, or Elvis Presley strumming
his Gibson guitar. But everyone is welcome here,
famous or not, at the historic Nu Wray Inn, where
the past and the present embrace one another like
the dearest of friends so often do before parting.

Brown Rabbit

A brown rabbit, its feet wet with dew, hops
around the yard. Nose twitching, whiskers waving,
it finds its way between the short grass
and the tall, skirting the place where copperheads
are known to curl, avoiding the open field.
Two hawks hunt here, a male and female. I saw
their brief coupling in the spring, how gently
he fluttered his wings against her feathers and flew
away, though he never wanders far from his mate.
But a rabbit knows nothing of the hawks' tenderness
and devotion. It flees from even the shadows
of their flying, furless bodies and sometimes dreams,
safe inside its burrow, of beaks and talons.

The Penguin

Oh my father who is dying—legs and belly
swollen, hands trembling—somewhere inside
your ravaged body is the boy who drove

his '35 Plymouth to his best girl's house
and after that, the Penguin. You told me once

the Penguin had the best burgers
in town, and milkshakes so thick you could eat

them with a spoon. Remember how you draped
your arm like a loose sweater across

my mother's bare shoulders? *I knew then*,
he said, *she was the one for me.* Now she waits

by your chair with pills to ease the pain
that dogs you like a playground bully. *Please,*

I pray, *let death be kind.* Let it come to him
like a front-porch-kiss beneath an arc
of light that follows him all the way home.

Mid-November

First, there is the dark through which the night birds
fly—barn owls, screech owls, whippoorwills, and loons.
Then the stars begin to fade, and the moon. And after

that, the sky brightens and the sun, hidden for so many
hours, peeks over the horizon. And from the core of its
burning body comes a pink haze that casts a roseate glow

over houses filled with people who can, even in sleep,
feel such joy. We would wake up singing if we could let
go for a while, of the weight of being human. So let us

rejoice in our light-kissed lawns and the bluing sky from
which the rosy blush recedes and the yellow light comes.
Listen to the whistle of black-capped chickadees, the coo

of doves. Marvel at the gilded trees and the burnished tips
of ryegrass. And remember—there is only this moment—
and while we're in the midst of it, what matters more than

deer running through the woods, patches of light that shift
and change over our own backyards, and the shadows of
songbirds moving faster than time across the chill ground?

Feast of Flowers

In response to Georgia O'Keeffe's "Ram's Head, White
Hollyhock-Hills"

Dreaming, I felt a brush press paint
into my skin. My body became

a hollyhock and after that, a pair
of horns, then hills. The artist's

face shone like a full Buck Moon,
the sleeves of her ebony dress

dotted with colors. Her breath was
warm and sweet, and all around

us there was sky and more sky—
so many shades of blue, only God

could count them. And on the sun-
baked ground: brittlebush, desert

lavender, chamisa, and chia sage—
a feast of flowers served in bones.

Grackles

Grackles have gathered below the bird feeder,
the oily, sunlit sheen of their bodies like shallow
pools of rainwater beneath a tire's rim of rubber—
their beaks like needles threaded with mealworms
and bits of seed-littered grass. To resent their brief
lives is petty and wrong, but I begrudge these birds
their greedy gobbling, the blithe ignorance of their
mortality. The image of my father fighting for every
breath, his throat like a tunnel collapsing, is super-
imposed over everything, even this. I can still see,
as if it was my own soul departing, the bedside vigil:
the bowed head of my grieving mother, the prone
body of my father, his lips turning bellflower blue,
his hands like objects artfully arranged on a linen-
draped table. A hospice nurse, for whom an old man's
death is as common as a cold, listened for the beat of
his heart and didn't find it. She looked stricken, and
I loved her for it as much I've loved anyone in my life.
But I cannot abide these funereal birds, the neat fit of
their folded wings, their cries like rusted gates, closing.

Four

Soleá

A tribute to flamenco dancer Soledad Barrio

Salome's dance started with seven veils, but Soledad
Barrio, fully clothed, is naked beneath the spotlight.
From the moment she appears, whatever

is not this woman—this stage, this *cantaor*'s plaintive
voice, the *palmeros* clapping, the intricate riffs
on the guitar—no longer matters.

Mesmerized first by her face, we watch her hypnotic
hands begin to undulate like sea anemones,
her supple, sensuous body telling a thousand tales

of passion and pain, rage and exile, her feet pounding
the floor like a barrage of cannon fire as she inhales,
exhales, her lungs working like a bellows.

She is magnificent and haunting, the embodiment
of *duende* as she dances like a Rom around a bonfire,
as if her life is a flame that will soon burn out.

Even Soledad's shadow is alive, pulsing with its own
beating heart, her body like a vein thick with heat
and blood until the final *braceo*—

her arms extended like the limbs of a twisted tree,
reaching beyond the limits of muscle, skin, and bone—
the stage hot enough, now, to birth a star.

In a Restaurant in Georgetown

Two men wearing business suits
sit at a small table. The man on the left
loosens his tie and smiles. The man
on the right smiles back. They begin to speak,
using only their hands, a language as swift
and silent as a flight of swallows.
People shout to be heard here,
but not them. They are an island of calm,
an oasis of quiet. Their tactile talk
is relaxed, natural—their faces unguarded.
In a world of sound, these men
share silence.

Kingfisher

White-collared like a priest, the belted kingfisher
has no mercy on its prey. Sporting a large, shaggy-
crested head and a dagger-like bill, it patrols the

shorelines of lakes, rivers, streams, and estuaries
like a rifle-toting guard, piercing the air with its
harsh, rattling cry. Mud minnows, sticklebacks,

crayfish, and tadpoles, beware of swimming in
clear water—watch the surface for a kingfisher's
shadow. Prior to its headfirst plunge, this top-

heavy bird with powder-blue wings and clerical
collar, seems benign as a butterfly. It hovers over
water like a hummingbird and its flower, its head

motionless, wings beating eight times per second—
with a tail designed to counterbalance its thick blue-
banded body. But the kingfisher's strike is lightning-

fast. In seconds, it catches its prey, beats it against
a branch by the riverbank, then flips the stunned
stickleback into its gullet like gourmet popcorn.

Open House

Driving down our street, we could feel
the hope, how it spooled away from our
car and wrapped around the house we
lived in for twenty-four years. Potential
buyers, who came and went for hours,
wanted this house to be the one for them
and so did we. But disappointment seeped
from the keyhole, lingered in the air of our
empty living room like a stranger's faint
perfume. Footprints dented the newly
vacuumed carpets, and crumbs from fresh-
baked cookies speckled the kitchen floor
we worked so hard to clean. The agent
smiled before leaving, assured us *it went
well* and *hopefully*, he said, *someone will
make an offer soon*. But disparaging words
like *no stainless steel appliances* or *too-small
master bath*, hang around long after they've
been said. So our unsold house looked as
forlorn as a middle-aged man whose blind
date walked into a bar and walked out, as if
she never saw his hand frantically waving.

Surfers

Slick as seals, a pair of surfers
with bronzed,

sway-backed bodies and sun-
bleached hair, stand

like young gods at the edge
of the shoreline,

their multicolored boards
dripping with seawater.

They watch the waves and we
watch them—not with

envy—because we, the middle-
aged and older, are content

to lie on a beach like ships
tethered to the dock. We know

life can break us. Every wave
could be the one to do us in.

Hawks

The red-shouldered hawk and his mate take turns
on a makeshift perch, surveying the field
for rodents. Like swivel rockers,

their feathered heads rotate in every direction,
with forward-pointing eyes black as underground
rivers. There could be no greater terror

in the tall grass than the blood-colored belly
of a red-shouldered hawk descending from the sky,
the pain of a sharp beak, tearing.

Still, they are magnificent birds—their checkered
wings like velvet cloaks tossed over the shoulders
of patrons of the opera,

and white-banded tails that flare like fans
when they fly. And the male's persistent cry, *kee-
ahh*, *kee-ahh*, can pierce the air

like an aria as it plunges towards its mate,
then up again, flying in wider and wider circles
until his final dive, wild with desire.

Blue Roan Gypsy Vanner Horses

You'd sooner find an arrowhead
in your grandma's put-up jars of
garden green beans than a Blue
Roan Gypsy Vanner Horse grazing
in your pasture. First bred by the
Rom for pulling caravans, they're
as uncommon as asperitas clouds
rolling in waves above the North
American plains and just as lovely
to look at, with their long manes
and feathered feet. Good-natured,
too, or so I've read, having never
seen one except in photographs
or while daydreaming that I am
not, (like I did the first time I rode
a horse), bouncing on its back as
if it were a mini-trampoline, but
matching the steady rhythm of this
rare roan's gallop—a horse so big
and blue, I might as well saddle
up the planet Neptune and ride it.

The Persistence of Memory

Of course, Dalí is my creation, said Gala
to one of her many lovers, a poor artist
she picked up in Catalonia. He found her

terrifying and voracious—a woman old
enough to be his mother. Still, he allowed

himself to be seduced. Perhaps it was her
marriage to his mentor that made her so

alluring. *What would Dalí be without his
muse?* she went on, as the young artist,

his body slick with sweat, lay panting.
He would be a nobody who paints soft

clocks, she whispered, and he understood
at last, *The Persistence of Memory*—the
feeling of exhaustion, its flaccid watches.

Wild Turkeys

On this late-March morning, a flock of wild
turkeys runs across a roadside pasture,
kernels of ice pummeling their buxom bodies.
Blossoms, once frilling a chain of cherry
trees, fall into the wet street—and daffodils
bend low, their petals battered by sleet.
Alarmed by the sudden change in weather
and thwarted from their poult-making
purpose, the turkeys head toward the distant
woods. Perhaps these panic-stricken toms
and hens will huddle, beak to beak, beneath
the budding limbs until the storm passes.
But lost from our sight, we can't say for sure,
what the wild turkeys did—only that they
were here, and now they are gone.

Red Dahlias

This steep hillside,
yellowed and shorn
of its tall grasses,

is dull as a dusty
floorboard except
where dahlias

grow. Redder than
raspberries, they
move like women

so lovely men
are afraid of them—
a floral flamenco

without sound. Yet,
the wind sings for
them and a screen

door claps as red
dresses swirl above
tender green ankles.

From Our House Behind the Churchyard, After a Storm

An hour after the storm, tree
limbs still sway, their green-leafed
twigs moving like the limbs

of swimmers in a sapphire sea.
Thunder booms in the distance
but they go on waving,

as if the lightning and the rain
are dear friends, departing. Beams
of brilliant light make gold

the ground and polish the branches
as puddles glitter beneath blades
of grass, silently sipping.

And high above the skittering
clouds, a red-tailed hawk circles
the churchyard, its wings

cupping the sodden, cerulean air
like a parishioner reaching
for a communal cup of wine.

How My Father's Death Colors Everything

Through condensation-streaked windows
I see the sun rising like cake in the oven, golden
and warm, and a doe runs along the ridge,
giving chase to the light. The sky may be a vault
filled with stars that only night can open, but for now,
there are slow-moving clouds as white and wispy
as an old man's beard. And catbirds fly low
above the sun-slicked grass as red-eyed vireos
play hide and seek, hopping from branch to branch
of the pin oak tree. If only a distant siren would cease
its wailing, like a child crying itself to sleep,
then my news-stained hands might rest easier
in my lap, and I could forget for a while,
that dark marauder stealing beloveds away,
one by one—how my father's last breath
rustled in his throat like leaves.

Five

The White Mountains in Early June

Sky-blue in the forefront, fading to cream
in the distance, the White Mountains
of New Hampshire rise from jade-green fields
and dark evergreen forests to merge on this overcast
day with low-hanging clouds. Hazed over by
some alchemy of air and light, these majestic peaks
and valleys could be living creatures, stilled
by sleep—a dreamscape filled by birch trees and red
spruce, alpine blueberries, and bog laurel.
And between the surging wind and birdsong,
the whine of swarming insects and the hiss of pine
needles gently swaying, there are pauses,
as if a breath is being held and then released,
perhaps the sigh of a lupine when the blue
butterfly finds its flower.

The River

Love me like the river loves the shore,
holding close its tattered banks, lacy with roots
and dirt. There is no thought to it, no need

for talking. There is only the rising mist,
the fading light. Listen. Do you hear
the humming of insects, the splash of a water

bird landing? I offer you these sights,
these sounds, as if this is enough to keep you.
Yet, you wind away from me like a river,

past beech trees and berry bushes, bare
feet slapping against a dock, and a lone whip-
poor-will, chanting its own name in the dark.

Three Turtles

Basking on a narrow log jutting over a lake,
three river turtles balance their warm, sun-dried shells
over brackish water as well as any acrobat, one
in front of the other, as if they're a trio of ducklings

waiting to cross the street behind their mother.
Not long hatched from their leathery eggs, by the look
of them, these turtles will live for thirty years
if they're lucky, which is longer than James Dean

but less than loggerheads, which live for fifty.
They have nowhere to be, no appointments, jobs,
or worries over money. There is only the dappled light
of the midday sun, the sound of dragonflies

hovering over the lake, the plop of a frog's belly
as it leaps into the murky water. Nearby, the bright coral
petals of a late-blooming azalea dot the ground like
embers, and the sky above them is the color of eastern

tailed-blue butterflies, without a cloud in sight.
And unlike people, turtles are never far from home—
no need for nostalgia or disappointment that the house
where they grew up looks nothing like they remember.

Instead, they carry their homes on their backs, moving
from place to place around the lake or in it—
wherever they wish to be—which for now is napping
on a log, and for river turtles, *now* is all there is.

Winter Landscape

Against a backdrop of darkening, snow-laden clouds,
a few rays of sunlight wrap their golden arms
around the bare limbs and trunk of an old oak tree.

It shimmers in the bright light like a crystal chandelier,
made more beautiful set against the slate sky
from which the snow is not yet heavy enough to fall.

How the land must long for the cool touch of flurries
on its yellow fields and dry, flaking soil.
And the rooftops of houses, still holding the heat

from a too-warm December, will soon receive
January's coldest kiss, and the weight of another winter
on their slopes and shingles, with silver plumes

of smoke billowing from the neighbors' chimneys.
And all the while, I sit by a window, looking out, near-
blinded by the dazzling bark of an oak

that was once a dull, greenish-gray. Yet, when the sun
has finished its brief moment of burnishing, the tree
will be gray again, then merge with the coming

night. Everything changes, and time is as fleeting
as the snow only now beginning to fall—each second
a small universe that flickers

and dies, faster than a child's sled on a sheet of ice.
But look at the light, how it fades like watered-down
paint into the purpling dusk.

Listening

In memory of Anya Krugovoy Silver

Listen. Flowers
are whispering.
A light is passing
by them that isn't
the sun. It is a light
created by a woman
saying good-bye,
her face pressed
against the fragrant
leaves and petals,
her lips moving
in songs or poems
or prayers—a soul
so brilliant, the stars
long ago gave her
a name. They are
calling it now and
look. She is going,
yet everything she
touches still shines.

Litchfield Beach

Arcing just beyond the waves, dolphins break
the surface of the sea. A lone osprey flies
toward its distant nest, a wriggling fish caught
fast in its talons, while a vivid image of my father
plunges headfirst into the water, his muscular
arms churning. Then, my grandmother,
long departed from this earth, baits her hook,
and my little brother, gone at twenty, carries his plastic
pail and yellow shovel to the shoreline. So many
ghosts of people I love on the beach, and with them,
a mirage of my six-year-old self, dark hair flecked
with sand and salt, and my mother lying on a lounge
chair, her face so smooth, only light could find
a place to land, never a shadow. Happiness
was ordinary back then, so we hardly noticed
it was there—nor the sorrow, waiting
like a fish hawk to swoop in.

Rose

Flower of love, your pinwheel petals whirl
with color. They are soft as a baby's feet,

the hollow in a woman's throat. Male and
female, ovaries and anthers, a rose needs

itself and no other, unlike swans and barn

owls and wolves that mate for life. Sweet
narcissist with your necklaces of thorns,
you grace our gardens, decorate our cakes.

We sip your hips, spray your scent on our

necks and wrists, strew your petals across
our beds. But a rose, in love with itself, is

soon spent, its stalk bereft of flowers, while
lovers can go on loving even if one is gone.

Walking with My Mother

We walk by a weathered old house
surrounded by trees, where the windows,
some without screens, are partially open.
Around the bend, a gray-haired woman works
in her garden, her spine curved like a scimitar,
one gloved hand raised in greeting. We wave
back, but keep going—the memory of my father
following us as close as shadows. We pass
parked cars, a yard strewn with toys,
a picket fence crowned by blue hydrangeas.
What a gorgeous shade of blue, I say.
My mother pretends to see it.

Crows

Under an ash-colored
sky, hundreds of crows
gather in an open field.

Some are standing still,
but most are hopping
as if the brown grass

is full of burning coals,
their caws a cacophony
of sound. The ground

is pulsing with long-
legged, big-bodied birds,
their bills and feathers

Elvis-hair black. And
look at how they take
flight in tandem,

then scatter—the way
grease splatters from
the same hot pan.

The River of Doubt

From our hand-hewn dugouts, we hear the screaming pihas, the calls of the red-eyed, blue-faced hoatzin birds, the chirps, trills, and buzzes of the yellow banded dart frogs trolling for mates. And though cicadas' hollow abdomens amplify their songs, our empty bellies clench with hunger and we are silent.

With supplies low in the Roosevelt-Rondon Expedition, we navigate the mysterious River of Doubt as it twists and winds through uncharted rainforest, its waters rife with piranha, pit vipers, bull sharks, and anacondas. And flying through the moist air, swarms of sulfur butterflies covet our salty tears,

and disease-carrying mosquitoes bite. Survival is the goal for *camaradas*, so we paddle and pray, our dreams, when we can sleep, filled with monsters. But our Colonel, Candido Rondon, is focused and unafraid, facing jaguars, caimans, rapids, and starvation, unwavering in his resolve to complete the mission.

Courageous, though sick and injured, Roosevelt insists we leave him behind to save his son as well as ourselves, but we push on, with Native Peoples, the *Cinta Larga*, watching from the jungle. The Colonel speaks of them with admiration, even tenderness, leaves them presents by the river. Their dark eyes

remind me of *minha esposa*, my children, who I may never see again. But the light of a good man's spirit is brighter than the breast of the black-faced hawk, so perhaps Rondon will be the one to save us. His will, alone, might be strong enough, (though our party remains in constant peril), to keep us safe and alive.

Swan

A mute swan, the color of new snow,
seems to glide atop the shallow, tea-tinted
reservoir as if her heavy, longnecked body
is as light as lilies. With one leg tucked
onto the soft slope of her back, the other
paddles toward the duckweed and stonewort,
skirting trees that once stood tall, reduced
now, to rotting remnants. She is by far
the loveliest creature in this watery landscape,
her reflection a close second to her elegant,
ethereal beauty. With no mate in sight,
she swims across the roadside wetland,
her contented solitude a balm to passersby,
alone in our cars. We all have a place
in this world, she reminds us, where even
the beat of a single swan's heart
is an indispensable sound.

Home Alone

My husband has left for work, our daughter
grown and gone. Friends with their own
cares to carry, may or may not call.

Finally, I say out loud, my face can settle
into sadness, my body sag like an old

building sinking into the ground. I will wear
my grief like a favorite sweater with missing
buttons and frayed edges, its once vivid

color faded now, to gray. But the birds
won't stop singing, and frost looks like glitter

glued to the grass. On and on the sun shines
and the songbirds sing until the door

that sorrow slammed shut opens, and light
seeps like water into the dry crust
of my day, spoiling everything.

Six

Birch Trees

In the North Woods,
silver-barked birches
rise from the fern-
covered ground, each
branch on every tree,
a new configuration.
Dappled with morning
light, their triangular
leaves are fluttering
like hundreds of jade-
green wings, and birds
sing to one another
from high above our
heads, their songs the
word *joy* set to music.
So we speak in soft
voices, as if these
woods are an outdoor
cathedral, and every
birch tree, an offering.

Branch Point Fridays

for Leonard

In the crook of the couch's soft elbow,
we are settled in to watch another movie.
A lamp burns in the hallway, its circle of light
like a planet in our house, benign
as the moon. And there are streetlamps

glowing through the slats of all the blinds
in the front windows along with porch
lights from other peoples' houses.

The teenage boy two doors down
is probably shooting hoops in his darkened
driveway, and at least one dog is,

without a doubt, being walked. A siren wails
in the distance and grows louder,
then less so, which means it isn't coming
for our neighbors or for us. We are safe
here and warm, nestled

like small animals in the comfort of our home
even as a million terrors happen outside
our doors, including the barn owl's

hunt and the mice making a run
for it over an open field and all the rest
of what goes on, night after night,
which we won't think about until tomorrow.
For now, our bodies,

weary from the long day, have let go
of worries. We know the stars are shining
above our roof though we can't see

them, and the earth is spinning, but we
can't feel it. We are following
the lives of unreal people doing imaginary

things while we sit rib to rib, hip to hip,
your arm around my shoulders—twenty-nine
years of welding one body
to another until we are as inseparable
as conjoined twins, sharing the same heart.

Música Norteño

The subway doors open and in jumps a couple
of Mexican guys carrying guitars, grinning wider
than the gap between the glassy-eyed teenager
slumped in the corner with his ripped jeans and faded
t-shirt that says, *What are you looking at?*
and the gray-haired, thick-waisted businessman
clutching a leather briefcase like any minute, somebody
is sure to steal it. The guitar players' voices rise
like skyscrapers through the scarred ceiling of the subway
car, and it feels like the sun hitched a ride on the way
back down because their songs are bringing a lot
of light into this metal box. They collect
our appreciation in the form of a few dollar bills
tossed into a battered cowboy hat until the doors open
and the music-makers leap into the next car
so Security can't catch them, followed
by a harried mother with four kids who slide
into the bowels of the rain-soaked city
like a family of harbor seals.

Fish Hatchery

I remember those rectangular cement pools,
the slender, silvery backs of juvenile fish swimming
fin to fin in watery boxes—how our grandfather
propped his foot on the side as he leaned

over the edge, one elbow resting on his thigh,
his dimpled chin thrust forward as he peered into
the shallow water along with my brother
and me, our eager faces reflected on the glittering

surface. We watched the fish moving in tandem,
their tails swishing back and forth like Grandmother's
broom when she swept the front walk. It looked
like a fish ballet—their scales like sequins sparkling

in the Blue Ridge Mountain light, and the three
of us, a rapt audience—two small children
and their doting grandfather—and I, the only one
left who remembers the dance.

Ode to My Vacuum Cleaner

First, there is the comforting roar of cleanliness
as we glide together across a room, the sound so
loud it drowns out the neighbors' barking dogs,
the washer's spin cycle, and the machinations of
computers and appliances constantly humming
like bees hovering over flowers. My ears, in fact,
are ringing from the cacophony of dust, dirt, and
sock lint, not to mention whatever else might be
lurking between the threads of rugs and carpets,
being lifted away by you, my darling Hoover. But
I forgive you for your exuberance, your penchant
for finding loose change and lost objects dropped
on the floor—once, nearly pulling down a set of
blinds by their dangling cord, the plastic piece on
the end mangled beyond recognition. I have only
myself to blame, however, for steering you wrong
since it is my hand, alone, that dictates where, in
every room, the two of us will go. And have I told
you today, how much I admire the tracks you leave
behind so all who enter will know, for sure, that
our rugs and carpets are, if not completely clean,
at least clean-ish? I appreciate, as well, how you
are always ready for yet another whirl around the
house, as efficient as you were whatever year it
was, we brought you home. And though my push
and pull isn't quite as forceful as it used to be, you
never complain, but simply go on doing the thing
for which you were made. For this and more, my
vivacious vacuum, my hallowed Hoover, you have
my thanks, two dimes, and at least one gold earring.

Massage Therapy

for Gia

Hour after hour, my daughter labors
in low-lit rooms to calming sounds
of falling rain, flute music, or ocean
waves, kneading the flesh of strangers.
Her hands, coated with fragrant oils,
glide over aching muscles, her dark
hair framing her face like the folded
wings of a black swan, her attention
laser-focused on a client's latissimus
dorsi, trapezius, and rhomboids, labels
new to most. But we all know where
it hurts, how unkind words, jobs that
went to someone else, the loves we
have lost—lodge in our lower backs
and shoulder blades, our sore necks
and tight tendons. And we know how
good it feels when tension melts away,
the pulse of our pain slowed by some-
one who moves through this world like
a sun, sharing her warmth and her light.

Two Herons

At day's end, a heron and her mate
meet where a small island juts
into shallow water. Fading light ripples

across the lake's serene surface, turning
their russet beaks tangerine,

their wings a deeper shade of blue.
I think of you and me, the ebb and flow
of our lives, our long marriage. I love

how sunlight strolls down the hallway
of our house, touching our faces

with gentle hands as we sit together
in the evenings, talking—or stand as we
are now, watching herons hunt.

The Black Bear that Batted the Bird Feeder Across Felicia's Backyard

She is late this year, to hibernation, and the snow
is early, coating roofs and lawns, the surrounding
woods where a bear can always hide when there
is danger. But there is little to fear where the soft-
voiced woman sleeps and the moon is a sliver in
the night sky. And though she is a medium-sized
bear with short, rounded claws, she can huff, jaw-
pop, teeth-clack, woof, and moan while backing
away, her toothy snout more menacing than her
hefty, thick-furred haunches. Tonight, the stairs
are slick with ice and hard to climb, but the bear
still reaches the feeder. She gobbles up the seeds
and bats the empty box with her massive, wooly
paw, which sends it flying—then clamors down
the icy steps. Slipping and sliding, the bear blows
and clacks in case anyone is listening, but no one
comes. She'll be dreaming in her warm den when
the woman finds the broken feeder, a smattering
of seeds and hulls, and the tracks of a medium-
sized black bear pockmarking the pristine snow.

For Neil Young, Who Brings My Brother Back to Me

In memory of Thomas Martin Kirby, Jr., 1959–1980

Like a shadow puppet, your face,
Neil Young, isn't my brother's

face, but enough like it that I feel,
watching you sing, that he

is with me. I hear his voice inside
your voice—imagine

he isn't gone. Instead, he lives
in the house he didn't get a chance

to build, married to the girl
he never met. So let me thank you,

Neil Young, not only for your long
brown hair, but for picking up

that Martin guitar and soothing my
brotherless heart.

Red Berries

By an old wooden fence, clusters of berries
on the green-leafed Nandina plants were capped
this morning, with fresh-fallen snow. Chili-pepper
red, the berries' blush is a startling contrast
to the wedding-dress white of winter's latest blast.
For hours, the snow has fallen, each flake no larger
than a dime. How new it all looks, how bold
the berries beneath a sky as white as a snow-covered
field. And all along the sidewalk, the streetlamps
have long since lost the heat of their midnight
burning, and the roads are buried as if there are no
roads at all—as though these houses sprung
from the earth like buds unfurling, the way camellias
bloom in bitter cold. Without a soul in sight,
the ground opens its freezing arms to the down-tinted,
feathery flecks that will, when the temperature
rises, turn to water. But for now, we are icebound,
the berries a deeper red than they will ever be again.

Fog

Beyond a grass-covered hill as yellow
as nicotine-stained fingers, fog rises like smoke
swirling around the trunks and naked limbs

of the poplar trees. A pair of hawks cry out
to one another, and chickadees scatter,
their small bodies lighter than the sodden air.

All morning long, this fog has lingered
like it will never lift, as though some benevolent
god has softened forever, the world's sharp

edges. Deer have merged with the woods, birds
with branches, mice with the fields—as fog
moves across winter-weary lands

like a stampede of silent, silver-coated horses,
the sound of their hoof beats muffled
by muddy ground. Yet, above our sheltering

roofs, the sun is hiding behind a wall of clouds,
and all around it, invisible stars still shine.
So let the fog go on dangling like lace

from the pearl-gray sky, blurring and blending
the miles between us, until there is nothing
left of missing you, but the taste of rain.

Mockingbirds

It is a cold spring but still, the mockingbirds
are mating. They dance around each other,
flapping their flashy white-patched wings,

hopping up and down between blades of new
grass. He has sung to her his sweetest song,

and she has answered. Soon, there will be
eggs to hatch, and babies to feed. But this
moment is all about them—how they join

together, four wings fluttering and fluttering.
And just before parting, they dance a final

minuet before the female flies to the fence,
her mate to the feeder, their soft *hew-hews*
tender, their feathered bodies still quivering.

Afternoon Nap

At midday, light is a living presence
in the room. Warm and yellow, it butters my body

like toast as the ceiling fan whirs
and a sprinkler in the backyard sprays the tender

blades of new grass in rhythmic
bursts. My eyelids flutter like twin butterflies

until the colorful comforter, the bed and dresser
and chairs, all disappear—and every dream

is sweet. And when I wake, it feels like floating
to the surface of a sunlit lake where the water birds

wade, and the clouds above them race
across the sky like sloops.

What Matters

What other people think of you,
what they say, are burdens
no one should carry. Lift a spoon,

a cup, things that fit in your hand.
Carry on a conversation,
pick up a baby. Listen to the wind

when it whispers, nothing else.
There is no one watching you,
no one straining to hear what

you say. The present has arrived
and you are in it. Your heart
is pumping. Your breath moves

in and out of your lungs without
anyone's help or permission.
Let go of everything else. Let

your life, handed to you through
no effort of your own, be all
the proof you need. You are loved.

Acknowledgments

Thank you to God for His love and mercy. Thank you to my travel companion, most ardent supporter, constant friend, and husband of twenty-nine years, Leonard Folke Erickson—*Jag älskar dig*, darling. Thank you to my late mother and father, Tom and Loretta Kirby, for all they gave me and for all they taught me, and my late brother, Tommy, without whom my childhood wouldn't have been nearly as much fun. Thank you to my daughter, Gia, heart of my heart, and her loving fiancé, Brandon, and to my wonderful uncle, artist Stephen White. To the friends who continue to be so present, supportive, and caring in the heartbreaking aftermath of the death of my adored parents—thank you for never making me feel broken. My deep appreciation to Kevin Watson and Press 53, to the editors who have published my work, and to the talented authors who so generously wrote blurbs for this book. And thank you, dear readers. Much love to you all.

Terri Kirby Erickson is the author of five previous collections of poetry. Her work has received multiple honors, including the Joy Harjo Poetry Prize, Nautilus Silver Book Award, Atlanta Review International Publication Award, Gold Medal in the Next Generation Indie Book Awards, Nazim Hikmet Poetry Award, and many others. She was also selected to be in *The Sixty-Four: 2019*, featuring the best poets of 2019, by Black Mountain Press and *The Halcyone*. Her poems have appeared in Ted Kooser's "American Life in Poetry," *Asheville Poetry Review*, *Atlanta Review*, *Connotation Press*, *Healing the Divide: Poems of Kindness & Connection*, *JAMA*, *Latin American Literary Review*, *O.Henry Magazine*, *Plainsongs*, *Poetry Foundation*, *Poet's Market*, *storySouth*, *The Christian Century*, *The Sun*, *The Writer's Almanac*, *Valparaiso Poetry Review*, *Verse Daily*, and numerous other journals, anthologies, and publications. She lives with her husband in North Carolina.

Cover artist Stephen White specializes in figurative paintings done on wood in gold leaf and transparent oil glazes. His work is available through City Art Gallery in Greenville, North Carolina, and Gerrie & Co. at University Mall in Chapel Hill, North Carolina.

www.ingramcontent.com/pod-product-compliance
Lightning Source LLC
Chambersburg PA
CBHW021507090426
42739CB00007B/514